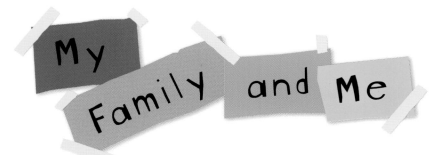

My Family and Me

Sharing
a Meal

Mary Auld

W
FRANKLIN WATTS
LONDON • SYDNEY

We all need to
eat to stay well.
We often share
a meal with
our family
when we eat.

? Your turn...

What meal did you
last share with
your family?

We share different meals during the day. We eat breakfast in the morning.

66 Leo says...

"Dad, Rosie and **I** like an egg for breakfast!"

In the middle of the day
we have lunch.

" Bryn says...
"Mum and I like salad for lunch.
My baby brother just has milk!"

In the evening, when everyone is home, Hiresh and his family sit at the table and share a big meal.

? Your turn...

What meal do you like in the evening? Where do you eat it?

Everyone can help get a meal ready. Simone and Ethan are making lunch with their mum and dad.

In the summer, Jake helps his dad with the barbecue.

Jake says...

"**I** love barbecues. You have to be careful not to burn yourself, though."

Mealtime is a good time to talk.

? Your turn...

What do you say at a meal when you ask for something or someone gives you something?

We have to clear up after a meal. Karl always helps his gran with the washing up.

Sometimes it's nice
to have a snack in
front of the TV.

? Tina says...

"Mum lets us have our tea
watching telly if we've had
a busy day and we're all a
bit tired."

On a sunny day, we can share a meal outside - a picnic. Anil's family go to the park for picnics.

? Your turn...

Where do you like to go for picnics with your family?

Families often eat out at restaurants. John and his mum have a burger when they go shopping.

When Jia's granny comes to stay, she takes Jia out for a treat.

Jia says...

"Granny is brilliant with chopsticks. She's teaching me how to use them properly, too."

We have lots of meals to celebrate with our families. Everyone loves food at a birthday party!

? Your turn...

What special events do you celebrate with a meal?

Some meals mark special events in a religion.

Many families have a feast on Christmas Day, when Christians celebrate Jesus's birthday.

66 Daniel says...

"My grandparents always come to our Shabbat meal. It's a time for the family to be together."

Jewish families share a meal on Friday night at the start of Shabbat, their day of rest.

What is your favourite family meal?

Some things to do

Plan a meal for all the members of your family. What time of day will it be? What will you eat? Write or draw a menu for the meal.

Do you know what 'table manners' are? With your friends, talk about manners and any rules your family has about meal times.

Make a list of all the different things that need to be done before, during and after a family meal. Which ones can you help with?

Write a poem or tell a story about the best family meal ever.

About this book

The aim of this book is to give children the opportunity to explore what their family means to them and their role within it in a positive and celebratory way. In particular it emphasises the importance of care and support within the family. It also encourages children to compare their own experiences with other people, recognising similarities and differences and respecting these as part of daily life.

Children will get pleasure out of looking at this book on their own. However, sharing the book on a one-to-one basis or within a group will also be very rewarding. Just talking about the main text and pictures is a good starting point, while the panels also prompt discussion:
• Question panels ask children to talk directly about their own experiences and feelings.
• Quote panels encourage them to think further by comparing their experiences with those of other children.

First published in 2007 by
Franklin Watts, 338 Euston Road
London NW1 3BH

Franklin Watts Australia
Level 17/207 Kent Street
Sydney NSW 2000

Copyright © Franklin Watts 2007
A CIP catalogue record for this book is available from the British Library.
Dewey classification: 642

ISBN: 978 0 7496 7626 1

Series editor: Rachel Cooke
Art director: Jonathan Hair
Design: Jason Anscomb

Photo credits: Paul Barton/Corbis: cover, 17. John Birdsall/John Birdsall Photography: 3, 8, 11. Paul Doyle/Photofusion: 14. Chris Fairclough/Franklin Watts: 10. S & R Greenhill : 5, 16, 19. Judy Harrison/Photofusion: 4. Michael Keller/Corbis: 9. Ute Klaphake/Photofusion: 20. Jenny Matthews/Franklin Watts: 21. Maggie Murray/Photofusion: 6-7. Anna Peisi/zefa/Corbis: 22. Superstock: 13.
Every attempt has been made to clear copyright. Should there be any inadvertent omission please apply to the publisher for rectification.

Please note that some of the pictures in this book have been posed by models.

Printed in China

Franklin Watts is a division of Hachette Children's Books, an Hachette Livre UK company.